To

From

Date

Beautiful

Valued

Empowered

Holy

Validated

Worthy

Equipped

Equipped

Unique

Wonderful

Wonderful

Blessed

Positioned

Beautiful

Valued

Empowered

Remembered

Validated

Trusted

Worthy

Equipped

Not Forsaken

Precious

Wonderful

Set Apart

Blessed

Blessed

Set Apart

Wonderful

Holy

Chosen

Equipped

Valued

Validated

Unique

Loved

Empowered

Beautiful

Positioned

Beautiful

Valued

Empowered

Remembered

Validated

Trusted

Worthy

Equipped

Not Forsaken

Precious

Wonderful

Set Apart

Blessed

40 DAY DEVOTIONAL

SILENCE THE ENEMY | TAKE AUTHORITY

TAKE YOUR Voice BACK

LEANDREA HOLLIDAY DRIVER

BIBLE REFERENCES:
AMPLIFIED BIBLE. ZONDERVAN, 2015.
ENGLISH STANDARD VERSION (ESV). CROSSWAY, 2001.
MERRIAM-WEBSTERS COLLEGIATE DICTIONARY. MERRIAM-WEBSTER
NEW INTERNATIONAL VERSION (NIV). BIBLICA, 2011.
NEW KING JAMES VERSION (NKJV). THOMAS NELSON, 1982.

OXFORD ENGLISH DICTIONARY, 2ND EDITION. OXFORD UNIVERSITY PRESS, 1989

AZLYRICS AZLYRICS.COM. AVAILABLE AT:
HTTPS://WWW.AZLYRICS.COM/LYRICS/TODDDULANEY/NOWEAPON.HTML
(ACCESSED: 26 SEPTEMBER 2023)

COBBS LEANORD, NATASHA TAMEIKA, ET AL. "TASHA COBBS LEONARD (FT. NICKI
MINAJ) – I'M GETTING READY." GENIUS, UNIVERSAL MUSIC PUBLISHING GROUP,
KOBALT MUSIC PUBLISHING LTD., 2017, GENIUS.COM/TASHA-COBBS-LEONARD-IM-
GETTING-READY-LYRICS.

FURTICK, STEVEN, ET AL. "SHALL NOT WANT." ELEVATION WORSHIP, 2021,
WWW.ELEVATIONWORSHIP.COM/MUSIC/SHALL-NOT-WANT.

HESLER, JONATHAN D, ET AL. "NO LONGER SLAVES." BETHEL MUSIC, BETHEL MUSIC
PUBLISHING (ASCAP), 2014, BETHELMUSIC.COM/RESOURCES/PEACE/NO-LONGER-
SLAVES.

HILLSONG WORSHIP & BROOKE LIGERTWOOD - WHO YOU SAY I AM LYRICS |
AZLYRICS.COM." WWW.AZLYRICS.COM,
WWW.AZLYRICS.COM/LYRICS/HILLSONGWORSHIP/WHOYOUSAYIAM.HTML.
ACCESSED 12 SEPT. 2023.

HILLSONG WORSHIP – NEW WINE (LIVE) (NO DATE) GENIUS. AVAILABLE AT:
HTTPS://GENIUS.COM/HILLSONG-WORSHIP-NEW-WINE-LIVE-LYRICS (ACCESSED: 25
SEPTEMBER 2023).

JIREH. WWW.ELEVATIONWORSHIP.COM/MUSIC/JIREH.

JOBE, KARI, ET AL. "THE BLESSING." ELEVATION WORSHIP, 2020,
WWW.ELEVATIONWORSHIP.COM/MUSIC/THE-BLESSING.

ISBN: 9798853172593

Table of Contents

Table of Contents

Introduction

I can't seem to get it right
I'm too damaged
God can't use me now....not after this
Who would want to listen to me?
Is He a good God?
I hate feeling this way.
What's the point of living?...

Are these thoughts haunting you?

Could you imagine what would happen if we gave
the enemy free reign in our minds, allowing him
to seize control of us through these suggestions
and reroute God's plans for us in the process?

Friend, I don't want that for us. If you find yourself
speaking or thinking like this, I encourage you to
stand firm in your identity and authority in Christ.
We have much work to do, and we've been given
the tools to combat these suggestive thoughts. It's
time to use them.

You're Invited

All too frequently, we give others' expectations of us and the pressure of our own fears and insecurities access to silence our voice. However, I want to inspire you to reclaim your power—be your true, authentic self—and embrace the liberty to express your beliefs, dreams, and desires unapologetically. The person God created you to be is the one this world needs, and you are deserving of being that.

I want to invite you on the path of rediscovery.

As we boldly pursue God's purpose and plan, let's commit to releasing the bonds of self-doubt and fear. Daily readings, reflections, and declarations will explore the transformative power of accepting our authentic selves and our God-given abilities to show up as His vessels.

Salvation

Luke 15:10 (AMP) *says, "In the same way, I tell you, there is joy in the presence of the angels of God over one sinner who repents [that is, changes his inner self—his old way of thinking, regrets past sins, lives his life in a way that proves repentance and seeks God's purpose for his life]."*

If you want to rededicate your life to Christ, or if you haven't yet done so, I urge you to take a moment to say the following prayer:

Heavenly Father,
I acknowledge my sinfulness and request your forgiveness. I believe you sent your son, Jesus Christ, to die on the cross for my sins and that it is through his sacrifice that I can have eternal life. Today, I choose to turn away from my sins and surrender my life to you. I ask that you come into my heart and be my Lord and Savior. I invite you to guide me, direct my path, and help me grow in my relationship with you. I pray that you will help me to live a life that honors you and brings glory to your name.

In Jesus' name, I pray. Amen.
Be Empowered. Be Encouraged. Be Equipped.

**Before we jump in,
let's declare this together:**

I declare that every lie of the
enemy is silenced in my life.
I will not suffocate under false
statements or succumb to his
tactics. I speak against every seed
illegally planted in my life.
The blood of Jesus covers and
defends me.
I surrender to God and trust Him
to reshape and reposition me.

With that being said, Let's get
started.

Awaken

John 8:12 (ESV): "Again, Jesus spoke to them, saying, 'I am the light of the world. Whoever follows me will not walk in darkness but will have the light of life."

Here's the tea: In my effort to "help God," I planned out what I wanted my life to look like. The Pinterest board was beautifully designed, and the vision was written down. However, I didn't consider the lessons necessary for my development.

I was building on the principles and expectations of society and my own desires, but not solely on God's purpose and will for my life. Sure, I thought about it, but did I depend on it? No, not really. I felt I needed something more "tangible" than what I read in the Bible. Because of this, we shouldn't rely on our feelings to guide us - only God can do this.

After my plans failed repeatedly, I found myself in a position where I needed to surrender to God. I had to give him an honest shot without anyone else's influence. This was a process, believe me. Sometimes, I felt my passion and creativity had died, and I had nothing to offer God. There were times when I couldn't hear His voice. However, I had to endure the process.

This was my awakening.

I remember Mark 5:21–43 when Jesus raised the little girl from the dead. After everyone declared her death, Jesus stated, "She is only sleeping." He advised them to believe in His ability to change the situation rather than be afraid, and today, I'm praying for that on your behalf.

You may have felt dormant as if your creativity was dying and your passions were suffocating, but you're only sleeping.

Do you believe that God has the power to change the course of your life? Your perception will change if your beliefs change. Awaken and shine; you are a lighthouse. It's time.

Declare

Jesus is the light; whoever follows Him will never walk in darkness but will have the light of life. I choose to put my trust in Him. He will never leave me or forsake me. His light will shine upon me, and I will be a beacon of hope and love to those around me.

Jesus is the source of my strength and the anchor of my soul. His light shines within me, and His power and wisdom enable me to live a life of purpose and impact.

Reflection

Chosen

1 Peter 2:9 (NIV): *"But you are a chosen people, a royal priesthood, a holy nation, God's special possession, that you may declare the praises of him who called you out of darkness into His wonderful light."*

Our voices are a priceless gift from God but are easily taken for granted. Whether through speaking, singing, writing, or simply living out our faith daily, we can use our voices to bring hope, healing, and encouragement to a hurting world. Unfortunately, our desire for acceptance frequently masks our true voices.

We might think our message isn't significant enough or that our words are inadequate. But we must remember that God has preselected and prepared us for His purposes. He has given us His Holy Spirit to lead and strengthen us, and He promises to use even our weaknesses for His glory.

Today, I want to encourage you to embrace the voice that God has given you. Whether you feel confident or uneasy, bold or timid, know that God can use you in mighty ways if you are willing to take the leap of faith. Speak up, lend your ear to those who need to be heard, and share the love and hope of Christ with those around you. Your voice may be the one that someone needs to hear today.

Declare

I am chosen—a member of a royal priesthood, a holy nation, and a special possession of God. He has called me out of darkness and into His wonderful light. I declare His praises daily.

I embrace the unique voice and testimony that God has given me, knowing that He has equipped me for His purposes.

I will walk in godly confidence, knowing that He strengthens my weaknesses.

May my words and actions reflect God's love and grace, and may others be drawn closer to Him through each word I speak.

our plans are not His. We have to surrender what we want to receive what He has.

To choose in advance

God has preselected and prepared us for His purposes.

made ready for use

No

Matthew 5:37 (NIV): *"Let your yes be yes and your no be no."*

It shouldn't be a surprise that walking in God's will can be challenging when we are constantly pulled in different directions. However, there is a way to establish boundaries. Saying "no" can feel uncomfortable and even confrontational, but it is essential for protecting our identity and purpose in God.

The art of "no" is not about being negative or rejecting others outright. Instead, it is about being intentional and discerning about what aligns with God's plan for our lives. When we say "no" to things that don't serve or distract us from our purpose, we allow God to work powerfully.

Three helpful tips as you practice the art of "no":

Be clear and direct:
Saying "no" doesn't have to be rude or harsh. It's better to be clear and direct about your intentions. Use "I" statements and communicate your needs respectfully.

Trust your instincts:
Your gut instincts often indicate what God is leading you towards. Pay attention to the feelings and reactions that come up for you when you are presented with an opportunity or request. If it doesn't feel right, trust yourself to say "no."

Prioritize your purpose:
When you say "no" to something, you say "yes" to something else.
Prioritize and say yes to your purpose in God and consider
whether an opportunity will serve that purpose. If it doesn't align
with your calling, passing may be better.

Remember, saying "no" can be an act of love and self-care. When
you protect your identity and purpose in God, you can show up
more fully and authentically in all areas of your life.

Declare

I am a child of God walking in His purpose for my life. I
recognize the importance of saying no to protect my identity
and purpose in God.

I will be clear and direct in my communication, respectfully
sharing my needs with others. I trust my instincts and recognize
that they often signify God's leading in my life. I will prioritize
my purpose, saying "no" to things that don't align with God's
plan for my life.

The expectations of others or the distractions of this world will
not sway me. Instead, I will trust in God's guidance and lean into
His Holy Spirit for wisdom and discernment.

I am confident in my identity in Christ and my purpose in His
Kingdom. Saying "no" is not a negative act but rather a powerful
act of self-care and protection.

Quick Note

Remember that saying 'no' is not just a refusal; it's an act of self-care and empowerment. You reclaim your voice and control your life by setting boundaries and making room for what truly matters. Embrace the power of 'no' to say 'yes' to your own well-being and authenticity.

Remember this message as you continue to find your voice and live authentically.

Reflection

Decide

Hebrews 12:1 (NIV): *"Therefore, since we are surrounded by such a great cloud of witnesses, let us throw off everything that hinders and the sin that so easily entangles. And let us run with perseverance the race marked out for us"*

It is easy to get into the place of wanting something to change, shift, or grow, but we often fail to recognize the significant piece that will push this into activation mode: making the decision. My mother taught me that if you want to be or do something, you must decide to go after it. No more having one foot in and one foot out; that is how you lose your balance and create a space for chaos and confusion.

Let's pause for a moment
What are your desires and/or goals for the next three months?

_____

_____

_____

_____

_____

_____

_____

_____

_____

Where are you now?

_____

_____

_____

_____

_____

_____

_____

What steps can you take to reach your goals?

_____

_____

_____

_____

_____

_____

_____

What's distracting you?

_____

_____

_____

_____

Your desire to see change will happen when your decisions support your vision.

I encourage you to release anything that blurs, taints, confuses, or hinders where God is taking you. Cease the distractions; your future depends on it.

Take Action:
Wake up with purpose.
Walk with expectation.
Pray and worship as if it has already been done.
Surround yourself with people who build you up, challenge you, and motivate you.
Dream again and begin to create.

God has major plans for your life; it is time to get into position.
Make the decision, and make it well.

Declare

I lay aside every weight and sin that hinders me from running the race set before me.

I fix my eyes on Jesus, the author, and finisher of my faith.

I will press forward towards the goal, knowing His grace is sufficient for me. I will not grow weary or lose heart, but I will run with endurance the race set before me.

I am a conqueror, an overcomer, and a child of God.
Victory is my portion.

Reflection

Take Action

Wake up with purpose.

Walk with expectation.

Pray and worship as if it has already done.

Surround yourself with people who build you up,
challenge you, and motivate you.

Dream again and begin to create.

Position

Ephesians 2:10 (ESV): "For we are his workmanship, created in Christ Jesus for good works, which God prepared beforehand, that we should walk in them."

As believers in Christ, we are responsible for seeking out our purpose and walking in it. However, sometimes, we may not know where to start or feel stuck in our current situation. To fulfill our purpose, we must first get into position, which means:

Aligning ourselves with God's plan

Seeking His guidance in developing our gifts and talents

Preparing ourselves for what He has called us to do

Getting into a position is a process, not a destination. If we want to walk in our purpose, we must first seek God's will and direction for our lives. Prayer and meditating on Scripture are essential tools for this process. We must also take the time to evaluate our gifts and talents, as well as our passions and values, to determine how they align with God's plan for us.

Next, we must develop and sharpen our skills and abilities. This may require education, training, or mentorship. We must be willing to invest time and energy in developing ourselves and preparing for the opportunities God has in store for us.

Finally, we must be willing to step out in faith and take action. This may mean taking risks, facing challenges, and stepping outside our comfort zones. But obeying God's leading will give us the strength and courage to overcome any obstacle.

This is a process that requires continual growth and development, as well as a humble and teachable spirit. During this time, we'll come to know the art of preparation.

Declare

I am God's handiwork, created in Christ Jesus to do good works that He has prepared for me.

I choose to align myself with His plan and purpose for my life. I will seek His guidance, develop my gifts and talents, and work to prepare myself for what He has called me to do.

I will walk in humility and teachability, allowing God to grow and develop me constantly. I will step out in faith and take action, even when faced with challenges and obstacles.

I will significantly impact the world and bring glory to God's name through my obedience and faithfulness. I am chosen, equipped, and empowered to fulfill my God-given purpose. Amen."

Quick Note

As believers, we must understand that our purpose in life is not just to exist but to be a Change Agent for the Glory of God. That said, you are equipped with extraordinary gifts and talents to fulfill that plan. When we allow those gifts to serve others, we not only bring glory to God, but we also bring fulfillment to our own lives. It is through serving others that we can find true happiness and purpose.

So, let us strive to live out our God-given purpose by performing good works and using our gifts and talents to impact the world. Remember that we are God's creation and have a special role to play in His plan.

Reflection

Prepare

Proverbs 24:27 (NIV): *"Prepare your work outside; get everything ready for yourself in the field, and after that build your house"*

One of the greatest lessons we can learn from the Bible is the importance of preparation. God values preparation and takes it seriously. He prepared everything in the world before He created man. Jesus spent thirty years preparing to fulfill His assignment on Earth, and the apostles spent time preparing for the church's launch.

Preparation is important because it lays the groundwork for our success. Without proper preparation, we might achieve temporary success, but it will not last, and we may not be able to withstand the challenges that come our way.

Proverbs 24:27 tells us to prepare our work outside and get everything ready for ourselves in the field before building our house. In other words, we must ensure that our foundation is solid before building our dreams or visions. We cannot skip the preparation stage and expect to achieve our goals. This may include acquiring the necessary knowledge, developing new skills, and gaining experience. Simultaneously, we must invest time and effort into building our relationship with God, which will equip us with everything we need.

Since life is unpredictable, we must continue to be watchful and flexible after making the necessary preparations. The fact that we have planned and are relying on God to guide us through the difficulties allows us to persevere despite the fact that we cannot control unforeseen events.

Therefore, regardless of the season we're in, we must prioritize preparation to achieve lasting success. It's time to dedicate ourselves to the process, stay focused on the goal, and trust God's plan and provision.

Declare

I will prioritize preparation, knowing it is the foundation for my success. I will invest the time and effort to acquire the knowledge, skills, and experience I need to build.

I will seek God's guidance in every step of my preparation, committed to following His plan and purpose for my life.

I will remain vigilant and adaptable, knowing that life is unpredictable, but I trust God to help me navigate any challenges.

I will stay focused on my goals with perseverance and determination, trusting in God's provision and timing.

Neither fear nor doubt will drive me. I will face every challenge with courage and faith, knowing God is with me.

My preparation will not be in vain, for God will bless the work of my hands and cause me to prosper.

I'm Getting Ready

Tasha Cobbs Leanord ft. Nicki Minaj

Verse 1

Eyes haven't seen, And ears haven't heard
The kind of blessings, The kind of blessings
That's about to fall on me
'Cause victory is here, Kicked defeat out the door
God's doing a new thing, Get ready for overflow

Chorus

'Cause I'm getting ready (I'm getting ready to see)
Something I've never seen

Verse 2

Beach house vibes maneuver the jet ski 'cause I serve a God
that parted the Red Sea, Multi-million dollar commercials for
Pepsi, From food stamps to more ice than Gretzky.
I don't gotta talk; the Lord defends me, I watch them all fall
for going against me, 'Cause me and all my angels shot the
devil up. While you were trying to pull me down, I leveled up.
I leveled up twice, I leveled up three times. He tapped 'em and
told 'em, "She's mine." So even when I cried, I knew I'd be
fine. Prepared for a miracle blessing in these times. Now
praise Him, raise 'em, name it, claim it. Every tongue that rises
up against me shame it. I breathe success in and out of my
lungs. I got the power of life and death coming out my tongue.

Reflection

Let's Pray

Dear Heavenly Father,
We come before You with hearts full of gratitude and reverence.
We acknowledge that You are the source of all wisdom and
strength, and we seek Your guidance as we embark on a journey
to take our voice back.

Your Word in Proverbs 24:27 reminds us of the importance of
preparation in all that we do. We understand that this goes
beyond practical tasks and addresses the readiness of our hearts
and spirits. Grant us the wisdom to recognize the areas where we
need to cultivate strength, resilience, and courage. Prepare us,
Lord, to speak with kindness, love, and understanding, even in
the face of challenges and adversity.

May our voices be instruments of Your grace, peace, and justice.
Give us discernment to know when to speak and when to listen,
when to advocate, and when to extend a hand in reconciliation.
Let our words be a reflection of Your truth and love.
Fill us with Your Holy Spirit so we may boldly and confidently
declare Your truth and share Your message of hope.

We commit this journey of preparation to You, trusting that Your
guidance and provision will be with us every step of the way. We
thank You for the opportunity to take our voices back and use
them for Your glory.
In Jesus' name, we pray.
Amen.

Unbecome

Ephesians 4:22–24 (ESV): *"to put off your old self, which belongs to your former manner of life and is corrupt through deceitful desires, and to be renewed in the spirit of your minds, and to put on the new self, created after the likeness of God in true righteousness and holiness."*

In this scripture, we see Paul calling us to put on our new selves, created in righteousness and true holiness. This transformation is not a one-time event but an ongoing process of growth and renewal. We must continually put off our old selves, which are rooted in sinful behavior and attitudes, and replace them with the new character that Christ develops in us. Simply put, getting rid of the carnal mindset is the first step toward becoming Kingdom-minded. This mindset aligns with God's truth, which requires seeking God through prayer and studying His word.

To obey God's commands, we must fight against our natural inclinations. This can be challenging, but we can draw strength from the Holy Spirit, who empowers us to live a life pleasing to God.

Ultimately, our transformation is a reflection of Christ's work in us. As we put on the new self, we grow to be more like Him, and His love and grace are made manifest in our lives. This transformation is not just for our own benefit but also for others who will see us as a touchpoint for Christ.

What do you want to let go of?

_____

_____

_____

_____

_____

_____

_____

_____

_____

Now, give yourself permission to walk away...

Next, encourage yourself to step forward. Do this by stating who
you are in Christ. Encourage yourself in Him.

_____

_____

_____

_____

_____

_____

_____

_____

_____

_____

_____

_____

On a separate Sheet, write your Personal Mission Statement. Here are a few guiding steps below to get you started:

Seek the Kingdom of God
Spend time praying and seeking God's wisdom and guidance as you create your mission statement.

Reflect
Take a moment to think about your experiences, values, and the insights gained throughout this devotional. Consider how you've grown and what God has revealed about your purpose.

Identify Values
What values and principles are most important to you?

Purpose
Consider the following questions:
Who has God called you to be?
What unique gifts and talents do you possess?
How can you use these gifts to serve others and glorify God?

Combine your values, purpose, and aspirations into a concise and inspiring mission statement. Keep it clear and write it down.

Declare

I am called to put off my old self, which is corrupt according to my own sinful desires. I choose to be renewed in the spirit of my mind, allowing God's truth and His Spirit to transform the way I think and live.

I am putting on the new self, created in righteousness and true holiness, reflecting the character of God to those around me. I choose to live my life in accordance with His will, seeking to bring honor and glory to His name.

I am committed to the transformation process, knowing it takes time and effort. I will spend time in prayer and reading the Bible, allowing God's truth to penetrate my heart and mind. I will seek out other believers who can encourage me and hold me accountable as I seek to grow in my faith.

I declare that I am an agent of transformation in the world around me. As I am transformed, I will reflect on God's love and grace, pointing others to the hope that can be found in Jesus Christ.

I declare that I am living in righteousness and true holiness, reflecting the character of God in all that I do. I choose to follow Him wholeheartedly and to be an example of His love to the world around me.

New Wine

Hillsong Worship

Verse 1

In the crushing, in the pressing
You are making new wine
In the soil I, now surrender
You are breaking new ground

Pre-Chorus

So I yield to You and to Your careful hand
When I trust You, I don't need to understand

Chorus

Make me Your vessel, make me an offering
Make me whatever You want me to be
I came here with nothing but all You have given me
Jesus, bring new wine out of me

Verse 2

In the crushing, in the pressing
You are making new wine
In the soil I, now surrender
You are breaking new ground
You are breaking new ground

Chorus (1x)

Bridge (x2)

Where there is new wine
There is new power
There is new freedom
The Kingdom is here
I lay down my old flames
To carry Your new fire today

Chorus

Reflection

Complacency

Revelation 3:15-16 (NIV): "I know your deeds, that you are neither cold nor hot. I wish you were either one or the other! So, because you are lukewarm—neither hot nor cold—I am about to spit you out of my mouth."

Complacency is a formidable adversary. It silently creeps into our hearts, dulling our passion for God and numbing our spiritual senses. It causes us to settle for the status quo and be content with a lukewarm faith. However, the Lord desires so much more for us.

In the book of Revelation, Jesus speaks to the church in Laodicea, highlighting their lukewarm attitude. He wishes they were either hot or cold, meaning He prefers complete devotion or straight rebellion instead of half-heartedness.

Complacency leaves us stagnant, hindering our spiritual growth and stifling our witness for Christ. We may find ourselves attending church and going through the motions of worship, yet our hearts remain distant from God. We might read the Bible occasionally but fail to apply its truths. We become content with our achievements in the past and forget to press on toward greater things for God's kingdom. Don't allow complacency to take root in your life.

Take your voice back from complacency by doing this:
Examine Your Heart: Take a moment to introspect and assess your spiritual temperature. Are you fervent in your love for

37

God, or have you allowed complacency to seep in? Be real with yourself and with God in this evaluation.

Pursue God: Draw near to God through prayer, worship, and meditating on His Word. Ask the Holy Spirit to ignite a passion for Him and renew your desire to pursue His will.

Embrace Spiritual Discipline: Cultivate a disciplined lifestyle of prayer, Bible study, and fellowship. Seek accountability from fellow believers who can encourage you to remain steadfast.

Serve Passionately: Rediscover your calling to serve others. God has uniquely gifted you to make a difference in this world. Step out in faith and serve with passion, sharing the love and grace of Christ with others.

Remain Humble: Guard against pride, which can lead to complacency. Recognize your dependence on God and the need for His grace and guidance.

Remember, complacency is not irreversible. Through the power of the Holy Spirit, we can break free from its grip and rediscover our fervent love for God. Let us be a people who are passionate in our pursuit of God, resolute in our faith, and zealous in fulfilling His purposes on earth.

Declare

Simply put, I will not allow the spirit of complacency to be evident in my life. It shall have no roots here, nor shall it be familiar with the dealings of my future.

I will protect my flame of fire for the Lord.

Take Action

Today, let's reject complacency and embrace growth. Don't settle for comfort when God has extraordinary plans for you. Step out, face challenges, and pursue greatness. Rise above mediocrity and reach for your God-given destiny.

Stay motivated, stay hungry.

Reflection

_____
_____
_____
_____
_____
_____
_____
_____
_____
_____
_____
_____
_____
_____
_____
_____
_____
_____
_____
_____
_____
_____
_____
_____
_____
_____
_____

Vulnerability

Jeremiah 17:9 (NIV): *"The heart is deceitful above all things and beyond cure. Who can understand it?"*

Reflecting to assess who and where we are can be challenging and uncomfortable. We must be willing to look at our faults, weaknesses, and shortcomings. Additionally, we must be vulnerable with ourselves and with God.

This is significant because we require God's assistance in understanding our hearts to expose the areas that require transformation and to bring healing and renewal. Self-awareness and humility are critical.

I pray that we will have the courage to confront ourselves honestly as we seek transformation through God's grace. Let's put our faith in His love and power to effect genuine change in our lives and lead us to live in a way that exalts Him and brings glory to His name.

Declare

I choose to face myself honestly and to be open to the work of God in my life.

I am willing to be vulnerable with God and others and seek feedback and support as needed.

I am committed to the process of transformation, and I trust in God's love and His power to bring about real change in my life.

I choose to turn away from the patterns of this world and to renew my mind through His Word and His Spirit. I believe that through His grace, I can become the person He created me to be— a reflection of His character and His love in the world.

Self-awareness and humility are critical.

Reflection

Surrender

Luke 9:23–24 (ESV): *"And he said to all, "If anyone would come after me, let him deny himself and take up his cross daily and follow me. For whoever would save his life will lose it, but whoever loses his life for my sake will save it."*

It is essential to submit to Christ and be willing to let go of our desires and self-serving goals in order to truly find our voice. By doing so, we acknowledge that our identity, sound, and purpose are solely found in who He is.

In doing so, we'll embark on the freedom that comes from living for a greater purpose. We no longer have to strive to prove ourselves or seek validation from others. Instead, we find our worth and validation in Christ alone.

I encourage you to yield, submit, and surrender.

Declare

I will surrender my plans, desires, and voice to Christ. I know I will find true freedom and purpose when following Him.

I choose to deny myself and take up my cross daily, knowing that in doing so, I am following in the footsteps of my Savior. I trust that His plan for my life is greater than anything I could imagine, and I surrender my voice to Him, knowing that He will use it for His glory.

I reject the lies that tell me my voice is weak or insignificant, and I declare that my voice is powerful because it comes from Christ. When I surrender to Him, He gives me the courage and strength to speak up and share His love with those around me.

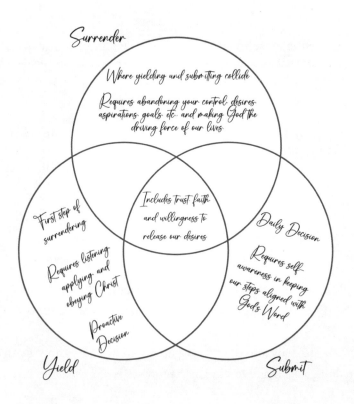

Surrender

Where yielding and submitting collide

Requires abandoning your control, desires, aspirations, goals, etc. and making God the driving force of our lives

Includes trust, faith and willingness to release our desires

First step of surrendering

Requires listening, applying, and obeying Christ

Proactive Decision

Daily Decision

Requires self awareness in keeping our steps aligned with God's Word

Yield

Submit

Reflection

Details

Matthew 6:30–33 (ESV): *"But if God so clothes the grass of the field, which today is alive and tomorrow is thrown into the oven, will he not much more clothe you, O you of little faith? Therefore, do not be anxious, saying, 'What shall we eat?' or 'What shall we drink?' or 'What shall we wear?' For the Gentiles seek after all these things, and your heavenly Father knows that you need them all. But seek the Kingdom of God and his righteousness first, and all these things will be added to you."*

It's easy to believe that God is only concerned with the big issues. However, Jesus teaches us that God is concerned with every aspect of our lives, no matter how small. How much more does He care for us, His children, if He takes such good care of the wildflowers in the field?

We can find solace in the fact that God is involved in the details of our lives. He is concerned with the smallest details, such as what we will eat and wear. He anticipates our needs before we even ask. He assures us that He will meet all of our needs if we put His kingdom first.

47

I encourage you to trust God with the details. Rest in His peace and be content knowing that He's in control and that He has your best interests at heart. Leave tomorrow for tomorrow.
Take one day at a time...

Declare

I trust in the faithfulness and provision of my Heavenly Father. I believe He cares about every detail of my life, from the smallest to the greatest.

I choose to release my worries and anxieties about the future, knowing that my Father already knows all my needs. I will first seek His kingdom and live righteously, confident that He will give me everything I need.

I will not consume myself with worries and concerns, for I know that my Father has a plan for my life. I will trust in His provision for me and be at peace, knowing that He is in control of every detail.

I choose to seek His will and follow His guidance, trusting He will guide me in the right direction. I know that as I seek Him first, He will open doors and provide for my every need.

Rest in God
Be content
Leave tomorrow for tomorrow

Jireh

Maverick City Music & Elevation Worship

Verse 1
I'll never be more loved than I am right now
Wasn't holding You up so there's nothing I can do to let You down
Doesn't take a trophy to make You proud
I'll never be more loved than I am right now

Verse 2
Going through a storm but I won't go down
I hear Your voice carried in the rhythm of the wind to call me out
You would cross an ocean so I wouldn't drown
You've never been closer than You are right now

Chorus
Jireh You are enough(x2)
I will be content in every circumstance
Jireh You are enough

Verse 3
Don't wanna forget how I feel right now
On the mountaintop I can see so clear what it's all about
Stay by my side when the sun goes down
Don't wanna forget how I feel right now

Chorus

Bridge
I'm already loved, I'm already chosen
I know who I am, I know what You've spoken
I'm already loved, More than I could imagine
And that is enough

Reflection

Speak

Psalm 23:1-4 (NIV): *"The Lord is my shepherd; I lack nothing. He makes me lie down in green pastures; he leads me beside quiet waters; he refreshes my soul. He guides me along the right paths for his name's sake. Even though I walk through the darkest valley, I will fear no evil, for you are with me; your rod and your staff, they comfort me."*

Have you ever felt silenced by your life circumstances? Maybe there was a time when you began to doubt your value and your ability to use your voice. Unfortunately, many people go through situations like this on a regular basis, but the good news is that the Lord is there and watchful, ready to jump in and help us find our voice, take it back, and maximize our sound.

As we journey toward taking our voice back, we can look to the Psalmist's example. He acknowledges the Lord's presence in his life and expresses his needs and desires to the Lord. We too can express our needs to the Lord, knowing that He is listening and cares deeply. He invites us to cry out to Him boldly, without fear of judgment or condemnation.

We can walk in any season with confidence, victoriously. He restores our confidence, reminding us of the purpose and value that He has given us, and He helps us to share our voice with the world.

So today, if you have been feeling silenced by life's circumstances, remember that you have a Good Shepherd who is with you every step of the way. Cry out to Him; He wants to hear from you. Allow Him to restore you and guide you as you share your gifts with the world around you.

Let's pause for a moment
What's that one thing you've been wanting to share with God, but you felt the weight of guilt and judgment?

_____

_____

_____

_____

_____

_____

_____

_____

Now you said it to him...
Trust that He can do something with your vulnerability. Do not carry the weight of guilt, shame, or judgment any longer. Walk in boldness and freedom. It's yours.

Declare

The circumstances of life do not define me. I am a child of the Most High God, and He has given me a voice to speak up and share the gifts and talents He has given me.

The Lord is my shepherd. He leads me beside still waters, and He restores my soul. Even in the valley of the shadow of death, I will not fear, because He is with me. His rod and staff comfort me, and He prepares a table for me in the presence of my enemies.

The Lord is my comforter and my guide. He reminds me of my worth and my purpose, and He empowers me to speak up.

I reject the lies of silence and shame, and I declare that I have a voice that matters. I am called to make a difference in this world, and I will not be held back by fear or insecurity.

I choose to trust in the Lord's provision and guidance, knowing that He will lead me to green pastures and guide me in paths of righteousness for His name's sake.

Use Your Voice

Reflection

Study

Romans 15:4 (ESV): *"For whatever was written in former days was written for our instruction, that through endurance and through the encouragement of the Scriptures we might have hope."*

Sometimes you may feel like you're fighting a losing battle, but as this verse reminds us, we have hope because of the Word of God. Scripture is available to us so that we may be strengthened and encouraged to endure challenging circumstances.

When I was recently listening to a sermon, the pastor mentioned that if you ever want to know what God is saying, pay attention to what He has already said. Applying this viewpoint, I see that the Bible is replete with accounts of people who overcame enormous challenges while remaining devoted to God and standing up for their convictions. From David and Goliath in the Old Testament to Esther and Mordechai in the New Testament, we see people reclaiming their voices and standing up for what was right.

In the same way, we can draw strength and encouragement from these stories as we seek to take our voice back. We can learn from their examples and find inspiration in their perseverance, knowing that if they were able to overcome incredible odds, we can too. Study their lives and learn.

As you read the Scriptures and meditate on God's Word, I encourage you to look for examples of those who reclaimed their voice and stood up for their beliefs. Let their stories inspire you and give you hope as you seek your voice.

Declare

I will find hope and strength in the Scriptures by drawing inspiration from the examples of those who have gone before me, endured incredible obstacles, and remained faithful to God.

As I read the Bible and meditate on the Word, I will find encouragement and hope, knowing that if they could reclaim their voice, I can too.

I am not silent.

For whatever was written in former days was written for our instruction that through endurance and through the encouragement of the Scriptures, we might have hope.

Endurance - the capacity of something to last or to <u>withstand</u> wear and tear.

Encouragement - the action of giving someone support or confidence,

Hope - to desire with expectation of obtainment or fulfillment

Here are some of my favorite people to study...

Joseph

Joseph was sold into slavery by his brothers, falsely accused, and imprisoned in Egypt. However, through his faithfulness and God's favor, he became the second-in-command to Pharaoh, ultimately saving Egypt and his family from famine.

Moses

God chose Moses to lead the Israelites out of Egypt, facing numerous challenges. He confronted Pharaoh, witnessed the plagues, parted the Red Sea, and received the Ten Commandments. Despite his initial reluctance, Moses displayed unwavering faith and obedience throughout his life.

Esther

Esther was a Jewish queen who courageously approached King Xerxes to save her people from an evil plot devised by Haman. Through her bravery and God's intervention, the Jewish people were spared, and the holiday of Purim was established to commemorate their deliverance.

Job

Job was a righteous man who faced extreme suffering. He lost his wealth, family, and health yet remained faithful to God. Despite enduring hardship and questioning God, Job's faith prevailed, and God ultimately blessed and restored him.

Reflection

Participate

James 1:22-24 (AMP): *"But prove yourselves doers of the word [actively and continually obeying God's precepts] and not merely listeners [who hear the word but fail to internalize its meaning], deluding yourselves [by unsound reasoning contrary to the truth]. For if anyone only listens to the word without obeying it, he is like a man who looks very carefully at his natural face in a mirror; for once he has looked at himself and gone away, he immediately forgets what he looked like."*

Your participation is vital.

This was a difficult truth to accept when God showed me I was not participating. I said everything right, but my actions didn't match my words.

This verse reminds us that just reading or listening to God's Word is not enough. Every day, we must put it into practice. It is not enough to claim to be a follower of Christ; we must demonstrate our faith to others.

If we are to regain our voice truly, the truth of God's Word should be lived out, despite how difficult or taxing it may be. It's essential that we engage with Scripture's teachings and allow them to transform our lives.

On a scale of 1–10, how involved are you in your process?

1   2   3   4   5   6   7   8   9   10

Are you satisfied with this amount of effort?

Yes or No

Would God be satisfied with this amount of effort?

Yes or No

What can you do to improve your participation?

_____

_____

_____

_____

_____

_____

_____

_____

_____

_____

_____

_____

_____

_____

Declare

I will not be content with merely listening to the Word of God; I will be a doer of the Word. I will intentionally put into practice what I have learned so that I may live out my faith with confidence and integrity.

I will not be like someone who looks at himself in a mirror and then forgets what he looks like, but I will allow the truth of God's Word to transform me from the inside out. I will take my voice back by living out my faith in a way that is evident to those around me.

Noteworthy:
Live out my faith with confidence & integrity

Allow the truth of God's Word to Transform me from the inside out.

Reflection

Language

Ephesians 4:29 (NKJV): *"Let no corrupt word proceed out of your mouth, but what is good for necessary edification, that it may impart grace to the hearers."*

It's the wedding day for the special bride. The decorations are in place, music is playing, guests have arrived, the wedding party has walked down, and everyone is anxiously waiting for the bride to enter.

Doors open, and the flower girl is coming to prepare the way, but instead of fresh rose petals, she throws twigs and withered leaves. Can you imagine how uncomfortable the bride may feel presenting herself in that manner? Or how the groom may feel receiving his bride in that state?

This is how we present ourselves when we use broken or unfruitful language. Ugly language is no different than the twigs and leaves.

So, as the bride of Christ, how are you preparing the aisle through your words?

Our language can be incredibly powerful, and what we say and how we say it can have a deep impact on those around us or even our future. However, it can easily fall into unfruitful language patterns, such as gossip, complaining, or negative self-talk.

I encourage you to be mindful of the words you speak. Choose to speak words of life and encouragement to yourself and others. When we do so, we create a positive and life-giving environment in our relationships and the world around us. We become a source of light and hope rather than negativity and discouragement.

Be intentional in speaking words that produce good fruit.

Declare

I will not let any unwholesome talk come out of my mouth. Instead, I choose to speak words that build others up and reflect the grace and love of Christ.

I will not fall into the trap of using unproductive language patterns, such as gossip, complaining, or negative self-talk. Rather, I will be mindful of my words' impact on those around me.

Reflection

Persevere

Romans 5:1-5 (NKJV) *"Therefore, having been justified by faith, we have peace with God through our Lord Jesus Christ, through whom also we have access by faith into this grace in which we stand, and rejoice in the hope of the glory of God. And not only that, but we also glory in tribulations, knowing that tribulation produces perseverance, perseverance, character, and character, hope. Now, hope does not disappoint because the love of God has been poured out in our hearts by the Holy Spirit who was given to us."*

Perseverance is the key to holding on to hope, especially when we feel discouraged or overwhelmed. When we persevere in our faith, we can be confident that God works in and through us, even amid our struggles.

Our trials can help us develop perseverance, producing character and hope. As we persevere through difficult times, we become stronger and more resilient, with a deeper understanding of God's love and provision.

Declare

Through faith in Jesus Christ, I can access grace, hope, and peace, even amid trials and difficulties. I choose to persevere in my faith and in my calling to use my voice for good.

I declare that through perseverance, I will develop character and hope, knowing that God is working in and through me for His greater purpose.

I declare that when I face adversity or hardship, I will hold fast to the hope found in Jesus Christ. I will trust in His love and provision, knowing He is with me and will never leave.

No Weapon

Todd Dulaney

Verse I
Through the fire
Through the flood
Through the valley
Through the mud
I won't worry
I won't Fear

No weapon formed against shall
prosper (x2)

Repeat Verse I

Chorus (x2)

Bridge
And when I think that I can't make it
I'm reminded You won't fail
And when I think that I can't take it
I'm reminded You are Good

Chorus (until fade)

Reflection

Stretched

Isaiah 54:1-3 (NIV): "Sing, O childless woman, you who have never given birth! Break into a loud and joyful song, O Jerusalem, you who have never been in labor. For the desolate woman now has more children than the woman who lives with her husband," says the LORD. Enlarge your house; build an addition. Spread out your home and spare no expense! You will soon be bursting at the seams. Your descendants will occupy other nations and resettle the ruined cities."

While reading this scripture, I am reminded of the difference between a casual morning stretch and a warm-up stretch during a workout. Stick with me - I promise I'm going somewhere with this.

That first stretch feels amazing when you first wake up after being still during the night's sleep. It allows your body to release any tension or stiffness and kicks off your start for the day ahead. This stretch is typically gentle and relaxing, helping to ease you into your morning.

On the other hand, intentionally stretching during a workout is often more vigorous and focused. It can involve holding a stretch for a longer period of time or pushing the limits of flexibility to improve your range of motion. The purpose of intentional stretching is to help your body move beyond its normal capability. It requires a different level of effort and challenge to reach the goal.

72

In this scripture, We see a woman being purposefully stretched to see and reap God's promises. We see her as barren, desiring a child of her own. But God promises her that she will no longer be barren, that she will bear fruit and be fruitful in ways she never imagined. However, it took her being stretched in her faith for the promise to be fulfilled.

Shouting for Joy → learning how to praise
Enlarging her tent → making room for what is coming

When you're being stretched in that manner, there is a demand for something you carry. The stretching comes in place to extend you, widen, or lengthen you to reach your full potential. Not because it's something fun but because it serves as a prerequisite for your next level.

Throughout our lives, we frequently encounter moments that stretch us beyond what we thought possible. These defining moments occur in various aspects, unveiling themselves through the depths of loss, the weight of grief, or the challenges of illness. In the professional world, we may find ourselves burdened by never-ending demands, overwhelmed by the weight of responsibilities, and yearning for recognition that seems to elude us. Furthermore, on our spiritual journey, we may experience a sense of disconnection, as well as doubts about our purpose and uncertainty about the path we are meant to take.

Whatever the situation, God is always present and willing to stretch us. He wants to take our difficulties and use them for His glory. It does, however, entail surrendering to God and trusting in his plan and purpose for our lives. It requires us to step outside of our comfort zone and embrace the unknown, even when it appears frightening or uncertain.

In stretching, we find growth and transformation. We discover new depths of our strength and resilience. We learn to rely on God in new and powerful ways. We see how He can take the brokenness of our lives and turn it into something beautiful.

I encourage you to take a deep breath and reach for the promises. It's time to stretch.

Declare

I am ready to be stretched by God.

Like the woman in Isaiah 54, I declare I am no longer barren but fruitful. I will bear fruit in my personal life, my professional life, and my spiritual life. God has promised to make me fruitful in ways I never imagined possible.

I trust God's plan for me, even when it is uncertain or scary. I know that God will never leave me nor forsake me and that he is always with me, even in the midst of the stretching.

I declare that I am strong and resilient and that I will grow in new and powerful ways through God's stretching. I will embrace the unknown and step out of my comfort zone, for I know that in the stretching, God will take my brokenness and turn it into something beautiful.

So today, I declare my surrender to God's stretching. I place my fears, doubts, and limitations at his feet and trust in his promise to make me fruitful. I am ready to be stretched, and I am ready for the new growth and transformation that are to come.

75

Define Your Faith Stretching Goals:

What are some specific ways you'd like to stretch your faith?
These could be related to prayer, serving others, or
deepening your understanding of Scripture.
Can you write down about three goals?

_____

_____

_____

_____

_____

_____

_____

_____

Develop an Action Plan:

On the next sheet, I couldn't outline practical steps you can
take to work towards every faith-stretching goal. Next, break
these steps into manageable, actionable items.

Go for it!

Reflection

_____
_____
_____
_____
_____
_____
_____
_____
_____
_____
_____
_____
_____
_____
_____
_____
_____
_____
_____
_____
_____
_____
_____
_____
_____

Pressure - proof

Psalm 118:5–6 (AMP): *"Out of my distress, I called on the Lord; The Lord answered me and set me free. The Lord is on my side; I will not fear. What can [mere] man do to me?"*

Life has a way of putting us under immense pressure. However, as followers of Christ, we have access to a power that can render us pressure-proof.

Psalm 118 reminds us of the psalmist's unwavering confidence in God's faithfulness and protection. When the author felt hard-pressed and overwhelmed, their instinct was to cry out to the Lord. This is an important lesson for us as well. When life's pressures mount and threaten to crush us, our first response should be to turn to God in prayer, pouring out our hearts before Him.

Keep in mind that God's deliverance may not always look as we expect. It may not mean an immediate removal of the challenges we face. However, it does mean that God is present with us in the midst of our struggles, providing us with a place of refuge, comfort, and peace. When we trust in Him, He expands the boundaries of our hearts and minds, allowing us to see beyond our immediate circumstances and glimpse the greater work He is doing.

We have an unshakeable trust in God's deliverance. As you face the pressures of life, remember to cry out to the Lord. Seek His presence and trust in His deliverance. Embrace the spacious place He offers, allowing Him to expand your perspective and strengthen your faith. Declare confidently, "The LORD is with me; I will not be afraid." With God by your side, you can navigate life's pressures with unwavering trust and emerge pressure-proof, anchored in His unfailing love and provision.

What used to intimidate you is now about to work for you. Why? Because you're pressure-proof. Shift your mindset, renew your language, and take every obstacle as an opportunity to elevate.

Declare

I am pressure-proof, for I have the Lord on my side. When I face moments of distress and anxiety, I will turn to God in prayer, for he is always there to comfort and guide me. God will answer and free me from the chains of anxiety and stress.

I can live boldly and fearlessly, for I trust in God's strength and guidance.

I will remain steadfast in Him. My faith will NOT waiver. I reside in the joy of the Lord, and it is my strength. I will not faint amid adversity. I will not give up, give in, or surrender to what may challenge me.

I will rise above, for I was built to handle the pressure, and I will handle it well.

Reflection

Vigilence

John 10:10 (NIV): *"The thief comes only to steal, kill, and destroy; I have come that they may have life and have it to the full."*

More than ever, it's crucial for us to remain vigilant, guarding our hearts, words, and minds against the enemy's schemes. John 10:10 serves as a powerful reminder of the battle we face but also of the victorious life Christ offers us.

Jesus states that the thief comes to steal, kill, and destroy. The thief represents the enemy, Satan, who seeks to rob us of our identity, purpose, and voice. He uses various tactics to steal our self-worth, kill our confidence, and destroy our future, hindering us from living the life God intends for us.

However, Jesus proclaims a powerful truth: He has come that we may have life and have it fully. In Christ, we find the restoration of our voice, authority, and purpose. Through His sacrifice, we are empowered to walk in freedom.

To walk in authority and take our voice back, we must be vigilant. We cannot afford to be passive or complacent. We need to guard our hearts and minds, filtering out the negative influences and lies of the enemy. We do this by immersing ourselves in God's Word, praying, and seeking the guidance of the Holy Spirit.

Walking in authority also requires us to align our thoughts and actions with God's truth. We must recognize our identity in Christ [If you haven't already, you'll hear me state this a lot]. When we understand our worth and value in Christ, we can confidently speak and act in alignment with His will. We can boldly proclaim the truth, share our testimonies, and use our voices to make a positive impact in the lives of others.

As we take back our voices and walk in authority, we must also remember that we are part of a community of believers who can encourage, support, and sharpen one another. Together, we can stand against the enemy's attacks, edify one another, and amplify our collective voice for God's kingdom.

Let us be intentional in guarding our hearts, renewing our minds, and boldly reclaiming our voices. Through Christ, we can overcome the thief's attempts to steal, kill, and destroy.

I am reclaiming my voice and walking with authority! By the power of Jesus Christ, I will not allow the thief to steal, kill, or destroy my identity, purpose, or voice. I am vigilant, guarding my heart and mind against the enemy's lies. I align my thoughts and actions with God's truth, boldly proclaiming His love, grace, and hope.

I will stand firm in our faith, putting on the full armor of God and cultivating spiritual discipline to withstand the enemy's tactics.

Reflection

No Longer Slaves

Bethel Music

VERSE 1

You unravel me with a
melody

You surround me with a
song

Of deliverance from my
enemies

Till all my fears are gone

CHORUS

I'm no longer a slave to
fear

I am a child of God

VERSE 2

From my mother's
womb You have chosen
me

Love has called my name

I've been born again into
Your family

Your blood flows
through my veins

BRIDGE 1

I am surrounded by the
arms of a Father

I am surrounded by songs
of deliverance

We've been liberated
from our bondage

We're the sons and the
daughters

Let us sing our freedom

BRIDGE 2

You split the sea so I
could walk right through
it

My fears are drowned in
perfect love

You rescued me so I could
stand and say

I am child of God

Commissioned

Isaiah 61:1 (AMP): The Spirit of the Lord God is upon me Because the Lord has anointed and commissioned me To bring good news to the humble and afflicted; He has sent me to bind up [the wounds of] the brokenhearted, To proclaim release [from confinement and condemnation] to the [physical and spiritual] captives And freedom to prisoners.

We all have assignments to fulfill— tasks at work, responsibilities at home, or endeavors we feel called to pursue. As we work to achieve these things, we must remember that God has equipped us with everything we need.

Isaiah 61:1 reveals that God has anointed and commissioned us for specific purposes. Each of us has a unique calling and assignment to carry out in this world. We are privileged and responsible for trusting God's guidance and strength as we walk in our purpose.

Often, we may feel inadequate or ill-prepared for the tasks before us. However, we can find comfort in knowing God's Spirit is with us.

Let's pause for a moment

Reflect on the tasks before you. Recognize that God has entrusted them to you for a reason. With His anointing and commissioning, you are equipped to bring good news to the humble and afflicted, to bind up the wounds of the brokenhearted, and to proclaim freedom to the captives and prisoners. With His empowerment, you can accomplish anything you set out to do.

As you fulfill your assignments, keep your heart open to God's leading. Seek His presence and guidance each day. Walk with the assurance that He has equipped you for the tasks. With God by your side, you can navigate challenges, impact lives, and bring glory to His name.

Be alert, equipped, available, and focused.

Declare

I have been anointed and commissioned for this time. I will bring good news, bind up wounds, proclaim release to the captives, and free the prisoners as God instructs.

I am equipped to fulfill the assignments before me, for the Spirit of the Sovereign Lord is upon me.

I declare that I will not be overcome by inadequacy or doubt because the Holy Spirit provides everything I need to succeed.

I will make a positive difference in the world, fulfilling the purposes for which I was created.

Reflection

_____
_____
_____
_____
_____
_____
_____
_____
_____
_____
_____
_____
_____
_____
_____
_____
_____
_____
_____
_____
_____
_____
_____

Isaiah 61:1 (AMP): The Spirit of the Lord God is upon me Because the Lord has anointed and commissioned me To bring good news to the humble and afflicted; He has sent me to bind up [the wounds of] the brokenhearted, To proclaim release [from confinement and condemnation] to the [physical and spiritual] captives And freedom to prisoners.

Alert

1 Peter 5:8 (MSG): *"So keep a cool head. Stay alert. The devil is poised to pounce and would like nothing better than to catch you napping."*

Alert: quick to notice any unusual, potentially dangerous, or difficult circumstances.

To effectively take your voice back, you must first be alert. This means being aware of the spiritual battle taking place around you. The enemy is relentless in his attempts; By staying spiritually alert, you can discern the enemy's tactics and actively resist his influence.

Being of sober mind is another crucial aspect of safeguarding your voice. It means maintaining clarity and focus in your thoughts and actions. It involves guarding against anything that might cloud your judgment, such as negative influences or unhealthy patterns. By remaining sober-minded, you can make wise decisions and protect your voice from being compromised.

To maintain alertness and sobriety, it is essential to cultivate a deep and intimate relationship with God. Regularly spending time in prayer, studying His Word, and seeking His guidance will help you discern His voice amidst the noise of the world.

Remember, your voice matters. Through Christ, you have the

power to rise above the enemy's attempts to silence you. Stay alert, be sober-minded, and allow God to amplify your voice as you speak His truth.

I will not be distracted; I will be alert.

As a child of God, I declare that I am alert and sober, aware of the enemy's tactics in my life. I choose to guard my heart and mind against his attacks, and I will not be complacent or careless in my spiritual life.

I am intentional about prayer and reflection, seeking God's presence and wisdom in my life. I will cultivate healthy community and accountability, surrounding myself with other believers who can speak the truth and encourage me.

I will guard my thought patterns and behaviors, focusing on God's truth and promises rather than negativity and fear.

With God's help, I declare that I am strong and resilient against the attacks of the enemy. I will overcome his lies and schemes and live confidently and courage in Christ.

Reflection

Equipped

2 Timothy 3:16–17 (NIV): "*All Scripture is God-breathed and is useful for teaching, rebuking, correcting, and training in righteousness, so that the servant of God may be thoroughly equipped for every good work.*"

Equip: supply with the necessary items for a particular purpose

As followers of Christ, we are called to make a positive impact on the world around us. However, if we're honest, there are times when we feel unequipped to fulfill our purpose. In moments like these, it is essential to remember the truth revealed in 2 Timothy 3:16–17.

Scripture is one of the most powerful tools we have for equipping ourselves to make a positive impact. When we intentionally spend time reading and meditating on the Bible, we gain a deeper understanding of God's character, His purposes, and His ways. The Word of God provides us with valuable principles for living our lives in a way that honors Him.

In addition, we can further equip ourselves by pursuing personal growth and development. This may involve enrolling in courses, attending conferences or workshops, seeking out mentors or coaches, or learning new skills. By investing in ourselves, we become better equipped to serve and impact others effectively.

However, it is crucial to recognize that equipping ourselves goes beyond acquiring knowledge or skills. True equipping begins with cultivating a surrendered heart that is open to God's will and responsive to His leading. As we align ourselves with God's plan, we can trust that He will provide us with the necessary resources, opportunities, and discernment to fulfill His purposes.

I encourage you to take intentional steps, equipping yourself with every good work. Make it a priority to spend time in God's Word, allowing it to shape your thoughts, actions, and character. Pursue growth and development in areas that align with your calling, seizing opportunities to expand your skills and knowledge. Above all, seek to cultivate a heart surrendered to God, willing to be used by Him for His glory.

Be intentional, be persistent, and trust in His guidance. He will empower you to make a lasting difference in the lives of others.

Declare

I declare that I am thoroughly equipped for every good work through the power of God's Word. I acknowledge that all Scripture is God-breathed and useful for teaching, rebuking, correcting, and training in righteousness.

I will seek to gain a greater understanding of God's character, purposes, and ways. As a result, I will learn valuable principles for living my life in a way that honors Him.

I will actively pursue growth and development in my life, by taking courses, attending workshops and conferences, seeking out mentors and coaches, and learning new skills. I will invest in myself to become better equipped to serve others.

I acknowledge that being equipped is not only about gaining knowledge or skills; it is also about cultivating a heart that is surrendered to God and open to His leadership. I invite the Holy Spirit into my life to help me discern His will and His direction.

"All Scripture is God-breathed and is useful for teaching, rebuking, correcting, and training in righteousness, so that the servant of God may be thoroughly equipped for every good work"

- *Rebuke*: express sharp disapproval or criticism of (someone) because of their behavior or actions.
- *Correct*: put right (an error or fault)
- *Train*: teach (a person or animal) a particular skill or type of behavior through practice and instruction over a period of time

Reflection

Quick Note

Life comes at us in waves, and it's important that we know how to respond that causes atmospheres to shift in our favor. When we look through the pages of the Bible, we are met with the breath of God for every word that was spoken was breathed out by Him! That we may be complete and equipped for EVERY good work. I don't know about you, but I want to speak like God. I want to know that every word I utter is one that is on assignment and aligned with what He wants. Scripture is our compass, our source of strength, and our connection to God. Let us embrace the Word and allow it to equip us for the journey ahead, for in it, we discover the keys to a life of purpose, peace, and unwavering faith.

Available

Isaiah 6:8 (NKJV): *"And I heard the voice of the Lord saying, "Whom shall I send, and who will go for us?" Then I said, "Here am I! Send me."*

Available: present or ready for immediate use of available resources.

God is constantly inviting us to join Him in His redemptive work, to speak words of hope to the brokenhearted, and to be ambassadors of His Kingdom. However, being available requires surrendering our own agendas

Just as Isaiah responded to God's call with a heart of availability and willingness to serve without hesitation, we too must be ready to say, "Here am I." It is an invitation to lay aside our fears, doubts, and self-limitations, trusting in God's guidance and provision. When we make ourselves available, God provides the strength, wisdom, and resources necessary. We can rest assured that we are not alone in our journey, for God goes before us and walks alongside us.

As you take your voice back and embrace your calling, remember that availability is not limited to a one-time decision. It is an ongoing posture of the heart. Stay attuned to God's voice through prayer, reading His Word, and seeking His presence. Allow Him to shape your desires and mold your character according to His will.

Your availability is requested.

I am available to You. I am willing to follow wherever You lead, to do whatever You ask, and to be whoever You call me to be.

I echo the words of Isaiah, saying, "Here am I. Send me!" I place myself at Your disposal, ready and willing to fulfill Your purpose and plan for my life.

I declare that I have a heart of surrender, willing to release my agenda, and plans to follow Yours. I seek Your will above all else and trust Your guidance and provision.

With Your help and power, I am ready and equipped to carry out Your mission. May Your will be done in and through me for Your glory and honor.

Power Statement:
"Your availability is requested...
Now, make it personal.
Say: My Availability is requested

Reflection

Focused

Proverbs 4:25 (NIV): "Let your eyes look straight ahead; fix your gaze directly before you."

Focus: an act of concentrating interest or activity on something

It is a task in itself to stay focused. Notifications, news articles, competing thoughts, and the urge of social media constantly bombard us. Yet, as followers of Christ, we are called to set our sights on His will and purpose for our lives.

Proverbs 4:25 encourages us to keep our eyes fixed directly ahead, steering clear of the detours and distractions that await our attention. It does not mean we should be oblivious to the world around us, but rather that we must prioritize our focus on the things that truly matter.

One key to maintaining focus is having clarity of purpose. When we have a clear sense of our aim, we can establish boundaries that shield us from distractions. This may involve turning off our devices [I know, I know - it's going to be tough], limiting our time on social media, or setting specific goals to protect our time and energy. Additionally, we can intentionally choose what we allow into our minds and hearts, seeking inspiration and drawing closer to God through uplifting and edifying content.

When we lack focus, we risk falling into ineffectiveness and allowing the enemy to rob us of valuable opportunities.
I encourage you to commit to unwavering focus on God's purpose and plan for your life. Fix your gaze on Him and intentionally eliminate the distractions that seek to pull you away.

Declare

I am focused on God's purpose and plan for my life. I intentionally set my eyes straight ahead and fixed my gaze directly before me, refusing to be ensnared by the noise and distractions of this world.

I am intentional about eliminating distractions and creating boundaries to protect my time and energy.

I dismantle every attack or habit that strategically positions itself to pull me away from God's will and plan for my life. I walk in alignment with His timeline, fully embracing His purpose for me.

Reflection

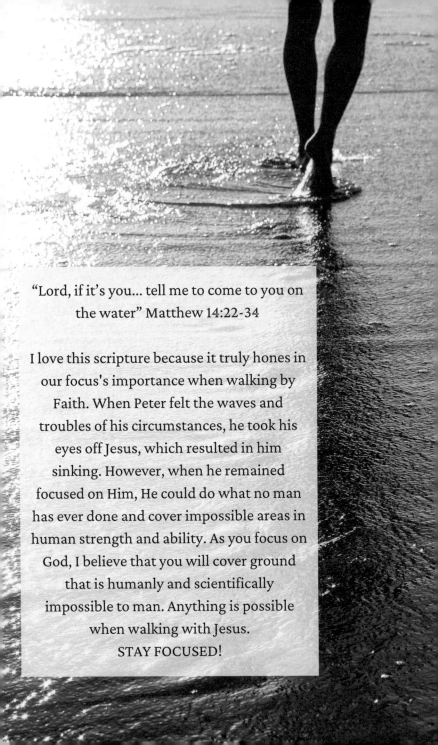

"Lord, if it's you... tell me to come to you on the water" Matthew 14:22-34

I love this scripture because it truly hones in our focus's importance when walking by Faith. When Peter felt the waves and troubles of his circumstances, he took his eyes off Jesus, which resulted in him sinking. However, when he remained focused on Him, He could do what no man has ever done and cover impossible areas in human strength and ability. As you focus on God, I believe that you will cover ground that is humanly and scientifically impossible to man. Anything is possible when walking with Jesus.
STAY FOCUSED!

Trust

Psalm 146:3-5 (NLT): "*Put not your trust in princes or in a son of man, in whom there is no salvation. When his breath departs, he returns to the earth; on that very day, his plans perish. Blessed is he whose help is the God of Jacob, whose hope is in the Lord his God.*"

It's tempting to trust in people or things that appear mighty and significant. We may feel pressured to associate ourselves with the "right" people or follow the latest trends in order to be accepted. While God will use people, or relationships, to introduce blessings into your life, it is He who makes it all possible. This Psalm reminds us that our ultimate source of help and hope should be in God alone

Human beings, no matter how powerful or influential, are ultimately mortal and limited. No matter how grand the plans, they will fade away. Only God is eternal and can truly save us from the trials and struggles of this life.

Trusting in God means anchoring our hope in Him above all else. It means acknowledging our own limitations and relying on His unwavering strength and divine guidance. It means recognizing that our ultimate success and security depend solely on His loving provision and faithful protection.

Let us resist placing our hope in people or fleeting things that will inevitably disappoint. Instead, may we be counted among the blessed, those who place their hope in the Lord their God. May we live lives that honor Him and bring glory to His name, both now and all eternity.

Declare

My trust and hope lie in Christ Jesus, the author and finisher of my days. I am fearfully and wonderfully made with a purpose uniquely designed for me. I shall be who He calls me to be, and I will have what He says belongs to me. I am solely dependent on Him.

My trust rests in God alone. I choose to put my hope in His unfailing love and limitless power, knowing that He alone can truly save and sustain me.

I make God my refuge and salvation, seeking His presence and relying on His faithful provision in all circumstances.

I am confident in God's promises and steadfast provision for my life. I trust that His plans for me are good and will provide me with the strength and guidance I need to fulfill His purposes.

My hope is secure, my trust unwavering, for my God is faithful and worthy of all praise.

Reflection

The Blessing

Elevation Worship ft. Kari jobe

VERSE 1
The Lord bless you And keep you Make his
face shine upon you And be gracious to you
The Lord turn His face towards you And give
you peace

CHORUS
Amen BRIDGE 1 May His favor be upon you
And a thousand generations And your family
And your children And their children And
their children

BRIDGE 2
May His presence go before you And behind
you, and beside you All around you And
within you He is with you He is with you

BRIDGE 3
In the morning, in the evening In your
coming, and your going In your weeping And
rejoicing He is for you He is for you

Amen

2 Corinthians 1:20 (AMP): *"For as many as are the promises of God, in Christ, they are [all answered] "Yes." So through Him, we say our "Amen" to the glory of God."*

Throughout the Bible, God has given us countless promises to stand on, and in Christ, every single one of them is a resounding "Yes." When we place our faith in Jesus, we become heirs to promises of salvation, healing, provision, guidance, and so much more.

Furthermore, God desires for us to receive and experience His promises in our lives fully - right now. He longs for us to walk in His goodness, faithfulness, and provision. This is why the apostle Paul declares in the scripture that "Amen" is spoken by us. We have an active role in receiving and declaring God's promises. As I frequently say, "We are in partnership with God."

The word "Amen" simply means "it is so." When we say it to God's promises, we express our agreement, alignment, and unwavering faith in His will. We boldly declare our trust in His power to fulfill every promise He has made.

Today, I encourage you to personalize God's promises by putting your name in them. Embrace the truth that you are a worthy recipient of His blessings. Don't disappoint God by failing to receive and utilize the abundant resources He willingly provides

///

for you. As you speak the promises of God, declare them over your life and circumstances. Your declaration of faith and trust in Him can transform your reality.

Declare

God is a promise keeper. His Word is filled with countless promises, and through my faith in Jesus Christ, I am an heir to every single one of them.

I receive and believe in God's promises for my life. I declare "Amen" to His faithfulness, goodness, and power to fulfill every word He has spoken.

I boldly speak out the promises of God, declaring them over my life and circumstances. My declaration of faith can bring transformation and align my reality with God's truth.

I will give God all the glory and honor as I experience the fulfillment of His promises in my life. I understand that His promises are not just for me but for the sake of His glory and the advancement of His kingdom.

Today, I reclaim my voice and boldly declare my trust in God's promises. I am confident that He will faithfully bring them to pass. In Jesus' name, Amen.

Bask in the Promises

He shall supply all of my needs according to Philippians 4:19.

I am not afraid nor dismayed. According to Isaiah 41:10, God is with me and will strengthen me. He will be my help and uphold me with His righteous right hand.

God will give me the desires of my heart as I delight in Him, according to Psalm 37:4.

God will not withhold any good thing from me, according to Psalm 84:11.

I do not lack wisdom; according to James 1:5, God generously provides it without reproach.

Reflection

Winning

Romans 8:37 (NIV): *"No, in all these things we are more than conquerors through him who loved us."*

This powerful declaration emphasizes that our victory is not just despite challenges but also in the midst of them. It speaks of a triumphant mindset that enables us to rise above circumstances and experience God's supernatural strength and grace.

The Bible contains accounts of individuals who achieved remarkable victories despite overwhelming odds. David defeated Goliath, Esther saved her people, and Daniel emerged unharmed from the lions' den. These stories remind us that our God is a God of the impossible, and He equips us to overcome the most daunting situations. The moral of the story is that we're winning!

Let's look at how to shift + apply this principle.

Perspective Shift: View challenges as opportunities for God to display His power and work in and through us. Trust that He can turn setbacks into comebacks and trials into triumphs.

Faith Shift: Ground yourself in the promises of God's Word. Meditate on passages that highlight His faithfulness, provision, and victory. Develop a deep conviction that nothing can separate us from His love and plans for our lives.

Power Shift: Take your hands off, and place it in the hands of the

Holy Spirit. by the Holy Spirit. He empowers us to face any obstacle, equips us with spiritual gifts, and strengthens our inner being to endure and emerge victorious.

Declare

In Christ, I am more than a conqueror. I have victory in every situation because of His love and power working within me. I refuse to be defined by my circumstances or limitations.

I embrace a mindset of triumph, knowing that God can turn any challenge into an opportunity for His glory. I trust in His promises and declare His truth over my life.

I am empowered by the Holy Spirit, who guides me, fills me with wisdom, and gives me supernatural strength. I rely on His leading and trust His provision.

YOU > Conqueror
See yourself BIGGER

Reflection

Heavenly Father,
We come before You with grateful hearts,
acknowledging and declaring the truth of Romans 8:37, that we
are more than conquerors through Him who loves us. Thank You
for the strength and courage You provide as we stand in our
authority of who You called us to be.

We recognize that there are times when life's challenges have left
us feeling voiceless, overwhelmed, and discouraged. In those
moments, help us remember that we are not defined by our
circumstances but by the unshakable love and victory we have in
Christ. With Your strength, we can rise above every obstacle,
every doubt, and every fear.

Grant us the wisdom to speak truth and love, to raise our voices.
May our words and actions reflect who You are.

Grant us the courage to overcome the self-doubt and fear that
often silences us. Fill us with the Holy Spirit, empowering us to
be light of hope, healing, and inspiration.

Let our voices be a testament to Your glory, showing the world
the power of Your transformative love.

In Jesus' name, we pray.
Amen.

Proverbs 25:28 (NIV) *"A man without self-control is like a city broken into and left without walls."*

Just as a city needs sturdy walls for protection and structure, we, too, require healthy boundaries to protect our identity, values, and well-being. Boundaries are vital for protecting our authentic voice and allowing us to navigate relationships, decisions, and challenges with clarity and self-control.

Proverbs 25:28 paints a picture that reflects a vulnerable city at risk of harm and danger. Similarly, our lives can become susceptible to chaos and compromise without self-control and healthy boundaries.

Let's pause for a moment.

Setting boundaries involves defining and communicating our limits, needs, and values. Here's how to implement it:

Reflect on Your Values:

Take a moment to identify your core values and beliefs. What matters most to you?

_____

_____

_____

_____

Identify Boundaries:

Where do you need to establish or reinforce boundaries?

_____

_____

_____

_____

_____

Communicate Clearly:

What do you need? What do you desire? When you can identify this, it helps explain the boundaries to others.

_____

_____

_____

_____

_____

Declare

With God's wisdom, I establish healthy boundaries in my life. I recognize that I am valued and validated in His eyes and deserve to protect my voice.

I surround myself with influences and environments that align with God's truth and purpose for my life. I prioritize relationships and commitments that support my growth and well-being.

I walk in self-control and self-awareness, making choices that honor my established boundaries. I communicate my needs and expectations with respect and assertiveness.

I embrace greater self-awareness, personal growth, and improved relationships by implementing healthy boundaries. God's love and guidance are with me in safeguarding my voice.

"A man without self-control is like a city broken into and left without walls."

walls = protection / safety. If there are no walls, a city is vulnerable and at risk for attacks.

Reflection

Excuses

Jeremiah 1:6-8 (ESV): "Ah, Lord God! Behold, I do not know how to speak, For I am only a young man. But the Lord said to me, do not say, "I am only a young man, Because everywhere I send you, you shall go, And whatever I command you, you shall speak. Do not be afraid of them or their hostile faces, For I am with you always to protect you and deliver you," says the Lord.

Excuses can hinder us from embracing God's call on our lives and living to our full potential. Whether it's fear of failure, self-doubt, or misplaced priorities, making excuses can prevent us from stepping into the abundant life and purpose that God has in store for us.

In Jeremiah 1:6-8, we see the prophet Jeremiah attempting to make excuses when God called him to be a prophet to the nations. Jeremiah claimed he was too young and incapable. However, God responded by assuring Jeremiah that his age or abilities were not obstacles because God would be with him, provide for him, and deliver him from any challenges he would face.

Can I encourage you? What you feel you lack will not disqualify you from doing the things God has called you to do. Trust in God to provide and direct you as you give Him your yes.

Declare

I trust in You completely to accomplish everything You have called me to do.

I declare that I am confident and courageous, knowing that You are with me every step of the way, ready to rescue me from any obstacles I may face.

I am capable of doing all things through Christ, who strengthens me. I refuse to let fear, doubt, or a busy schedule hinder me from pursuing Your plans for my life. With Your help and guidance, I will boldly step forward, fulfilling every purpose You have placed in my heart.

Empowered by Your Spirit, I will take risks, overcome challenges, and fulfill Your calling.

Thank You, Lord, for Your grace, strength, and leadership that enable me to stop making excuses and start living the abundant life You have for me!

Reflection

Shall Not Want

Elevation Worship & Maverick City Music

VERSE 1
Will You be my light, when I cannot see? When I can't take another step, Lord, would You carry me? When I've lost my fight, will You be my strength? Will You set me a table in the presence of my enemies?

CHORUS
I shall not want, I shall not want
Oh my soul's got a shepherd in the valley and I shall not want
I shall not want, I shall not want
Cause my cup's running over, running over and I shall not want

VERSE 2
I will lift my eyes to where my help comes from; And I won't be afraid of the shadow cause I've seen the sun. No I will not stop, when the way gets hard. Cause the green only grows in the valley and that's where You are

CHORUS

BRIDGE
I got goodness and I got mercy Hallelu, glory hallelujah
The Good Shepherd leads me to the waters Hallelu, glory hallelujah

He anoints me, anoints me with His oil Hallelu, glory hallelujah Now my cup is, my cup is running over Hallelu, glory hallelujah I won't fear, no, fear no evil Hallelu, glory hallelujah I will dwell in His house forever Hallelu, glory hallelujah Hallelujah hallelujah Hallelu, glory hallelujah

VERSE 3
When this life is over, I'm gonna live again Gonna trade this cross for a crown No, this is not the end When You call my name, I will take my rest There's a mansion in glory and You're gonna meet me there

CHORUS 2
I shall not want, I shall not want He will wipe every tear from my eyes I shall not want I shall not want, I shall not want I'll be home in His presence forever I shall not want For the Lord is my shepherd And I shall not want

Comparison

Galatians 1:10 (NIV): "For am I now seeking the approval of man, or of God? Or am I trying to please man? If I were still trying to please man, I would not be a servant of Christ."

Comparison is a common struggle that many people face. It breeds insecurity and can take away our joy and peace.

We live in a world where we are constantly bombarded with the lives of others through social media and other means, making it easy to compare ourselves. However, God has called us to set our minds on things above and to focus on who we are in Christ rather than according to the world's standards.

In Galatians 1:10, Paul reminds us that we should not seek the approval of men but rather of God. Our ultimate goal should be to please God and fulfill His purpose for our lives. When we turn towards Him, we can walk confidently in Him rather than seeking external validation.

Remember, comparing ourselves to others only leads to disappointment because we will never measure up to someone else's standards - we aren't supposed to. Instead, let's focus on our own journey and trust in God's plan for our lives. This doesn't mean we can't learn from others, but our focus should ultimately be on God's plan for our lives.

Declare

I will not compare myself to others or seek their approval, I will only seek to please God, for He has called me by His grace and I am fearfully and wonderfully made.

I will walk confidently with my own unique gifts and talents, knowing that they were given to me for a purpose. The opinions of others will not sway me, but I will trust in the Lord and His faithfulness.

So I walk in freedom from the bonds of comparison, and I will live a life that honors and glorifies God.

Note to self:
I've been validated
No longer seek approval

Where have you been comparing yourself?

_____
_____
_____
_____
_____
_____
_____

What does God say about this concerning you?

_____
_____
_____
_____
_____
_____
_____

131

Reflection

The One

Deuteronomy 7:6 (NKJV): "For you are a holy people to the Lord your God; the Lord your God has chosen you to be a people for Himself, a special treasure above all the peoples on the face of the earth."

Many of us have experienced moments of self-doubt, feeling as though we don't measure up or are undeserving of our current circumstances. We may harbor a sense of waiting for our true potential to be realized, for our chance to shine truly. These thoughts can damage our self-esteem and cause us to live in a constant state of insecurity.

Here's what I want you to remember:
God has chosen us as His treasured possession, which means we are valuable and loved no matter what. Our worth doesn't come from our appearance, achievements, or popularity. It comes from our position as children of God.

This truth is essential because it frees us from the fear and insecurity of negative thoughts. It allows us to embrace who we are and to live confident and fruitful lives.

When we understand our true identity, we live differently. We can boldly share our faith and stand up for what is right. We can be kind and compassionate to others, knowing that our worth doesn't come from how others treat us.

Recently, I was reminded that all my dreams and aspirations were given to me for a reason, and I had to decide to agree with God that I'm THE ONE to fulfill them.

So, I say to you, recognize that you are the one.
You're the one who can write the book.
You're the one who can stop generational curses.
You're the one that can have a successful marriage.
You're the one that can start the business.
You're the one who can be an example to those that's around you.

When negative thoughts come, address them with truth.

Declare

My worth and value come from my identity in God. I declare that I am holy and set apart, and that God has chosen me to be His treasured possession.

I take my voice back from negative thoughts and declare that I am valuable and important because I'm chosen.

Reflection

"God has chosen us as His treasured possession, which means we are valuable and loved no matter what. Our worth doesn't come from our appearance, achievements, or popularity. It comes from our position as children of God."

Heal

Psalm 147:3 (NIV): *"He heals the brokenhearted and binds up their wounds."*

We all bear the scars of past pain and heartache, whether from broken relationships, crushing disappointment, or deep-seated trauma. These wounds can linger in our hearts and minds, causing emotional turmoil and hindering our growth. However, God's tender love and infinite grace can bring healing and wholeness.

God is intricately familiar with our pain and heartache and longs to bring healing and restoration to our lives. This scripture serves as a reminder and a bold declaration of God's commitment to mend the brokenhearted and bind their wounds. To experience this healing, we must be willing to revisit and acknowledge the painful experiences that have shaped us. Is this tough? Yes! But we can trust that God's healing touch will restore and renew our hearts and minds.

Forgiveness is another crucial aspect of healing past wounds. By extending forgiveness to ourselves and others, we release the chains of bitterness and resentment that can keep us tied to our pain.

Try this
Reflect on past wounds, Pray for healing, Cultivate forgiveness, and seek community.

God's love is deep for me; he desires to heal brokenness.

I invite His healing touch into every area with complete faith and trust that He pays attention to the details.
May His restorative power make me whole again. I declare that I am forgiven, and I release burdens of the past.

His healing grace will guide me into a future filled with purpose and freedom.

By His stripes   I am healed

Reflection

Loyalty

Psalm 139:13-14 (ESV): "*For you formed my inward parts; you knitted me together in my mother's womb. I praise you, for I am fearfully and wonderfully made. Wonderful are your works; my soul knows it very well*"

Loyalty is a virtue esteemed throughout history and the scriptures; it serves as a foundation for strong relationships and commitment. Yet, in the quest to maintain this allegiance, we may unknowingly subject ourselves to a dangerous predicament: the muting of our own voices. This is where it becomes toxic.

When we unknowingly embrace toxic loyalty, we find ourselves trapped in silence. We may be afraid to voice our opinions, desires, or struggles, all in the name of not wanting to disappoint those we hold dear. Yet, in doing so, we inadvertently stifle the very essence of our God-given voice.

However, I want you to remember that God created each of us with a unique purpose and identity. Our voices, with all their authenticity, vulnerabilities, and strengths, are gifts bestowed upon us to glorify the Creator and impact this world.

God desires us to be devoted to one another in love, but not at the expense of losing ourselves. Instead, we are called to find strength in authenticity and vulnerability. Only when we are true to ourselves can we truly embrace the path laid out for us.

Embrace your voice, a powerful instrument of truth, compassion, and love. Seek to communicate openly and honestly with those around you, trusting that the bonds of genuine loyalty will only grow stronger when built upon a foundation of authenticity.

Declare

I declare that I am breaking free from the suffocating grip of lethal loyalty. I will no longer allow the fear of disappointing others to silence my voice. I embrace the freedom to express myself authentically and courageously.

I declare that I will establish healthy boundaries in my relationships. I will no longer sacrifice my well-being for the sake of loyalty. I will communicate my needs assertively and lovingly, respecting myself and others.

I declare that I will be genuine and authentic in all my interactions. I refuse to wear a mask of false loyalty, but I will be true to myself and others, fostering deeper connections built on honesty and trust.

I declare my gratitude for the gift of my voice. I am thankful for the opportunity to reclaim and use it for God's glory. I will cherish and nurture this precious gift, embracing its responsibility.

Reflection

Let's Pray

Lord, Thank you for the gift of life that you've given me. In your infinite wisdom and love, you formed every part of who I am. Thank you for making me unique, with strength, gifts, and abilities meant to bring you honor and glory!

God, when doubt creeps in, or the sirens of warning alert me, remind me of the truth in your Word. Let me never forget that your Word takes precedence over anything that I may experience. Let me not be loyal to the problem and the emotional response, but may I be mindful and loyal to the one who holds the answers.

Love

Psalm 51:10 (NIV): "Create in me a pure heart, O God, and renew a steadfast spirit within me."

A pure heart is a deeply desired attribute for every believer seeking a closer relationship with God. However, sin, tangled emotions, and worldly desires often cloud our hearts. Despite our shortcomings, God's infinite love and grace can purify our hearts and help us maintain our eyes on Him and love for His Word.

King David's cry for a pure heart reveals the natural longing etched within every believer's soul. Recognizing his humanity, David pleads with the Lord to create a cleansing work within him, restoring his spirit and allowing him to walk in alignment with God's will.

The journey for a pure heart begins with acknowledging our imperfections and the need for God's intervention. By confessing our sins and inviting His transformative love into our lives, our hearts gradually shed the impurities hindering our walk with Him.

Cultivating and maintaining a pure heart requires unwavering vigilance and discipline in our spiritual journey...

Continue to take your voice back by protecting your heart.

Declare

I walk humbly in posture, recognizing and admitting my imperfections before the Lord. I acknowledge that I am solely dependent on Him.

As I embark upon this journey, Prayer will be a priority of my days. I am committed to regularly communicating with God and inviting His Spirit to mold and shape everything concerning me.

God's word will be the foundation of my thoughts, desires, and actions - I will not part from what He has already said.

My life is His, and I trust Him to mature and reposition me as I find my voice and identity in Him.

Reflection

Wisdom

Proverbs 23:7 (NKJV): *"For as he thinks in his heart, so is he."*

The wisdom found within this text emphasizes the unforgettable connection between our internal thoughts and our outward realities. In order to live in alignment with God's will and reclaim your voice, it is essential to cultivate a renewed and transformed mind. The beliefs and attitudes we hold within our hearts ultimately determine our actions and perceptions of the world around us. This truth calls us to examine our thought patterns and their influence on our connection to God and one another.

Remember this: God desires us to experience abundant life. The path to this begins with a transformed mind - one that is continually renewed and purified to reflect God's own thoughts and heart. As we align our thoughts with His divine perspective, we can walk confidently in His will and experience the fullness of His blessings.

We do this by delving into the Word of God, where we engage with Scripture and allow it to reshape our thoughts, beliefs, and attitudes. As we meditate on His Word, our minds become increasingly saturated with His love and gifts for us.

Ultimately, by actively pursuing a renewed and transformed mind, we become more deeply rooted in God's purposes - for ourselves and His Kingdom.

Engage with Scripture: Dedicate time to reading, studying, and meditating on the Word of God, allowing it to reshape your thoughts and attitudes.

Depend on prayer: Cultivate a habit of prayer, inviting the Holy Spirit to convict and guide your mind in alignment with God's will.

Seek God-centered relationships: Surround yourself with individuals who can offer support, encouragement, and godly wisdom as you strive to transform your mind.

Practice self-reflection: Regularly assess your theought patterns, identifying areas where you must align your thoughts with the truth of God's Word. thoughts with the truth of God's Word.

Declare

I will embody wisdom in all that I do. I recognize that my thoughts, words, and actions have the power to shape my life and the lives of those around me. Therefore, I choose to align my mind with the wisdom of God and reject any negative and destructive thoughts.

I will seek the wisdom of God in all situations. I will intentionally seek His guidance through prayer, reading His Word, and seeking counsel from other believers.

I embody the qualities of wisdom, such as discernment, humility, and a teachable spirit. I will learn from my mistakes and use them as opportunities to grow and become wiser.

Reflection

Postured

1 Thessalonians 5:16-18 (NIV): "Rejoice always, pray continually, give thanks in all circumstances; for this is God's will for you in Christ Jesus."

Life's journey is often filled with highs and lows, joy and suffering, moments of triumph, and times of despair. Despite the ever-changing landscape of our circumstances, we are called to immerse ourselves in the continuous act of praising God. Recognizing His unwavering love, faithfulness, and presence can help us maintain a posture of gratitude and trust, even during the most turbulent times.

Our human nature often compels us to praise God when our lives are filled with blessings and to question His presence when we endure storms. However, 1 Thessalonians reminds us of the significance of maintaining an attitude of gratitude in every season of our lives. Praising God in the midst of challenging circumstances does not mean overlooking or trivializing our struggles. Instead, it is an act of faith, acknowledging the sovereignty and goodness of God even when life feels overwhelming. When we do this, we cultivate a more profound trust in His character. Our faith begins to mature and expand as we grow more reliant on His strength and less focused on our own limited understanding

Declare

I will rejoice always, even in the midst of trials and difficulties. I will hold onto the promise that God will never leave me nor forsake me. I will trust in His presence in my life, knowing that He is with me always.

I will pray continually, bringing all my worries and concerns before God. I will rely on His strength and guidance in all situations, knowing that with God, all things are possible.

I will give thanks in all circumstances, recognizing that God has a plan and purpose for me. I will trust that He is working all things together for my good, and I will thank Him for His mercy, grace, and love.

I am a voice of praise and encouragement, and I will use my voice to bring glory to God in all circumstances.

Reflection

Beautiful

Valued

Empowered

Holy

Validated

Trusted

Worthy

Equipped

Equipped

Unique

Precious

Precious

Wonderful

Wonderful

Empowered

Set Apart

Set Apart

Beautiful

Blessed

Blessed

Positioned

Certainty

Isaiah 55:8-9 (NIV): "My thoughts are not your thoughts, neither are your ways my ways...For as the heavens are higher than the earth, so are my ways higher than your ways and my thoughts than your thoughts."

Life is full of uncertainties, and it can be challenging to navigate through them. We often find ourselves facing difficult decisions, unclear paths, and unexpected challenges that leave us feeling lost and disoriented. However, as believers in Christ, we have access to a source of certainty that surpasses all human understanding. We serve a God whose ways are higher than our ways and who holds all things in His hands.

When we accept Jesus Christ as our Lord and Savior, we are adopted into God's family, and we become heirs of His promises. In Hebrews 6:18-19, we are reminded that because God cannot lie, we can hold tightly to the hope of His promises as an anchor for our souls.

As we embrace God's certainty, we can be confident that He is with us. This means trusting Him completely and surrendering our plans, dreams, and desires to His will, knowing He promises to direct our paths.

I trust in the wisdom of God, even when His ways seem mysterious, and His thoughts surpass my understanding.

I believe that He holds the universe in His hands and has a plan for my life that goes beyond my wildest dreams. I choose to surrender to His will and follow His lead, even when it requires me to step out of my comfort zone or confront my fears.

I will not try to confine Him to my limited perspective but instead seek to align my heart with His purposes.

Reflection

Isaiah 55:8-9 (NIV)
"My thoughts are not your thoughts, neither are your ways my ways...For as the heavens are higher than the earth, so are my ways higher than your ways and my thoughts than your thoughts."

Taste & See

Psalm 34:8 (NIV): *"taste and see that the Lord is good."*

To truly taste something, we must experience it for ourselves. We can read about food, look at pictures, and hear others describe it, but the only way to savor its flavors and textures is to taste it ourselves. Likewise, to understand wholeheartedly God's goodness, we must experience it firsthand.

In this scripture, David goes on to describe the ways in which he has personally experienced God's goodness in his own life. When he called out to the Lord, God heard him and delivered him from all his fears. Just like David, we can experience God's goodness in our own lives by calling out to Him. We can ask Him for help in our struggles, trust in His provision, and see His miraculous hand at work in our lives. Furthermore, don't miss the opportunity to share it with others. Just as we might recommend delicious food to our friends, we can share the goodness of God with those around us.

Declare

I will taste and see that the Lord is good. I will not be afraid to fully experience and enjoy His goodness in my life, for He has promised to bless me abundantly.

I choose to seek His presence in every moment of my life and to receive all the blessings He has for me - joy, peace, hope, wisdom, strength, and so much more.

Reflection

Authority

Luke 10:19 (AMP): "*Listen carefully: I have given you authority [that you now possess] to tread on serpents and scorpions, and [the ability to exercise authority] over all the power of the enemy (Satan); and nothing will [in any way] harm you.*"

This verse reminds us that as followers of Jesus, we have been given the authority to overcome the enemy's schemes and to speak the truth. However, it can be easy to forget this truth and fall into a mindset of defeat or powerlessness. But be encouraged! For we have been equipped with the power and authority of the Holy Spirit to overcome the enemy's attacks and to proclaim victory in the name of Jesus. We can trample on snakes and scorpions and overcome all his attempts to bring us down. We are not alone in this battle – we have the power of God within us.

How do we do this?

Root ourselves in the truth of God's Word and remind ourselves of His promises. Silence the lies of the enemy and hold fast to the truth that God loves, values, and empowers us.

Boldly speak truth into our own lives and the lives of those around us. Don't avoid difficult conversations or situations where the enemy is at work. Instead, we must stand firm in our identity as children of God and speak life into every situation.

Declare

I will not be intimidated or discouraged by the enemy's schemes,
but I will stand firm in the truth of God's Word and the power of
His Spirit.

I reject the enemy's lies and speak the truth into my own life and
those around me.

SILENCE THE ENEMY **TAKE AUTHORITY**
This world needs what God has put inside you.

Authority   the right to act in a specified way,
delegated from one person or
organization to another:

God, Himself, has authorized YOU.
Walk in your place of authority

Reflection

Luke 10:19 (AMP)
"Listen carefully: I have given you authority [that you now possess] to tread on serpents and scorpions, and [the ability to exercise authority] over all the power of the enemy (Satan), and nothing will [in any way] harm you."

Re Introduction

2 Corinthians 5:17 (NKJV): *"Therefore, if anyone is in Christ, the new creation has come: The old has gone, the new is here!"*

It's easy to feel defined by the labels and expectations that others place on us. We can forget who we truly are in Christ and start to believe the lies that we are not enough. However, when we believe in Christ, we are made new in Him. Our old self, with its sin and brokenness, is gone, and we are given a new identity as a child of God.

It's important to reintroduce ourselves to this new identity in Christ. We must speak truth into our lives and declare who we are in Him. We can say, "Hi, my name is [insert name], and I am a child of God. I am loved, chosen, and redeemed by Him. I am forgiven and free from the chains of sin and shame. I am a new creation in Christ, filled with His Holy Spirit and empowered to live a life of purpose and significance."

By reintroducing ourselves to this new identity, we are taking our voice back from the lies of the enemy and declaring the truth of who we are.

So at this moment, reintroduce yourself to your new identity in Christ. Speak truth into your life and remind yourself of your new creation in Him. Let His love and grace wash over you as you live the life He has called you to.

Declare

I am a new creation in Christ Jesus, and the old things have passed away. I choose to embrace the new life that He has given me and to leave behind the old patterns of thinking and behavior that no longer serve me.

My past no longer binds me, but I am free to walk in the purposes and plans God has for me.

I am worthy of love and acceptance, and I will no longer let the enemy's lies hold me back. I choose to walk in the truth of God's Word and declare that I am a chosen and beloved child of God with a unique voice and purpose that only I can fulfill.

Reflection

I'm Taking It Back

An original

In the presence of God, I stand tall,
Where His Spirit dwells, I give my all.
As I breathe in His grace, I'm reborn anew,
In the breath of God, His word rings true.

Every word He speaks, it's life, it's love,
From the heavens above, like a peaceful dove.
In His presence, I come alive, I thrive,
I'm taking back my life, and I'm taking back my drive.

With His word as my anchor, I'm unbreakable,
I rise above the storms; I'm unshakeable.
I'm taking it back, my life, my voice,
With the power of God, I'll be the force.

Are you ready for my reintroduction here,
shouting proud of who I am, both far and near.
A King's kid indeed, destined to rise,
I'm walking heavy and shining my light.

Conclusion

As we reach the end of this transformative journey, I encourage you to remember the importance of embracing the unique voice that God has given you and NEVER lend it to the works of the enemy. You were not called to confusion or to operate in fear. Stand confident in HIM and know that greatness is within you. Our voices hold the power to impact lives, share God's love, and become catalysts for positive change in the world around us - You cannot be silenced.

As you continue to walk with God beyond this devotional, commit to nurturing and cultivating your voice, knowing that it is a precious gift from the Creator. Remain rooted in your identity as a child of the Highest, and let your voice be heard, boldly proclaiming His truth, love, and grace to the world.

Lets Pray

Heavenly Father, we offer our heartfelt gratitude for this enriching journey through the Take Your Voice Back devotional. You have shown us the importance of using our unique voices to glorify Your name and impact those around us. We pray for the continued strength and courage to reclaim our voices, even in the face of fear and self-doubt.

As we move forward beyond this time together, we ask for Your guidance in every step we take. May we never forget the value of our voices, and may we use them to advance Your kingdom on earth. May our voices testify to Your love, grace, and transforming power.

MO

Thank you, Lord, for creating us with intention and purpose. We ask for the boldness to step into the calling You have for our lives, using our voices to bring light and hope into the world. In Jesus' name, we pray. Amen.

Go forth in confidence and faith, trusting in God's unwavering love as you reclaim your voice and make a lasting impact for His Kingdom.

Silence the enemy, and take authority!

Reflection

About THE AUTHOR

LeAndrea Holliday Driver is a multi-faceted individual with a deep passion for empowering others. As a devoted wife, mother, pastor, and coach, she brings a wealth of experience and understanding to her work. LeAndrea founded the "Take Your Voice Back Empowerment Revolution," where individuals are equipped to silence the enemy and step into their authority.

Born into a loving family, LeAndrea is the eldest of two children to Leamon and Angela Holliday. Her upbringing instilled a strong sense of faith and a desire to serve others. LeAndrea values the importance of family deeply and finds immense joy in partnering with her husband, Jonathan Driver, in ministry. Together, they lead Revitalize Ministries, an impactful organization based in Atlanta, GA.

With a heart to see people thrive, LeAndrea utilizes her extensive background in coaching, ministry, and leadership development to inspire and empower others. Through her various endeavors, she has impacted numerous lives by encouraging individuals to reclaim their voices and embrace their true identities.

Her commitment to faith, family, and empowering others has made her a well-respected figure in her community. This devotional offers invaluable insights, drawing from her personal journey and the transformative experiences she has witnessed throughout her ministry.